Midnight

Cover Design and Illustration: Madison Sanchez

First Edition: March 2019

ISBN: 978-1-7962-3068-0

Midnight

Poetry & Prose

Breanna C. Shievdayal

To the girl I've gotten to know within myself
over the last few years.
It's been a pleasure learning to love you

Author's Note

This book is a collection of my teenage years. That alone should inform you that it gets messy.

For the longest time I didn't know who I was writing for, the urge just came upon me at some of the best and worst experiences of my life. Through the bad times there was a voice in my head saying, "*Just write.*" The same happened through the good times. It wasn't until the very day that I finished putting this book together that I realized I was writing for myself, writing to cope and writing to give myself strength. I was winding and layering words around my heart, creating a nest so that even if it broke, the pieces would still be kept together.

In no way have I completely finished my journey and magically "become an adult" since the start of these poems, but I have learned quite a lot and grown in ways that I never imagined. My hope is that if you know firsthand just how messy life can get, these poems will help you to see that the stuff going on inside of your head isn't as crazy as it might seem.

There is no specific structure or categorization to these, just chronological (for the most part).

It is raw.

It is honest.

At times I felt like I was going crazy.

I hope you can use my nest of words as your own.

I hope this makes you feel more human.

This is now for you.

-BCS

June Jitters

I had a cup of coffee at 7:51 a.m. I felt it warm my throat and seep into my veins. It coursed through my body and made my heart jump, my tendons and muscles pulse and throb. If I closed my eyes and covered my ears, I could hear the blood rushing in my eyes, my heart rhythmically thump… thump… thumping away.

Maybe it had seeped deeper than just my veins, maybe it had found its way into my soul. After weeks of withdrawal, weeks of pulling away from my addiction, the minute I allowed it to access my body, it found a way to take over the most vulnerable and hidden part of me.

It made every inch of my skin pulse and yearn for more, because underneath it all, I wanted it; I craved it. It was better than any drug. My insides jumped and exclaimed, made their enjoyment evident. Outside, I was completely unfazed, aside from nervously shaking my knee. I had learned to repress it by then. For so long it was a part of me.

Through the late nights at concerts that made your heart vibrate, mixing it with candy and chocolate to a marathon of horror movies, sipping it for minutes at a time underneath the fairy lights by a window watching the snow fall, or perhaps as a silhouette in the computer light as I vigorously typed another sentence in my essay.

And now?

It wanted a way back in.

It wanted to join me as I crammed more information into my head and daydreamed about listening to waves crashing on a beach or seagulls calling out to each other in the air.

I can still taste it on my tongue, feel it in my heart, and recognize its weaving path through my veins.

Let Go

Gatsby loved Daisy for five years. Jim loved Pam for eight years. Yet theirs are love stories different from most others; they were written into existence.

- *It's time to let go*

Time is not a measure of love. Love is on an entirely different scale that nothing else could possibly compare to. Love is measured in the stolen glances while she is focused on her work. It is measured in the way she smiles without fail every time he instinctively runs his hands through his hair. Love is little, yet it makes us feel so big.

Gorgeous/Soror

Your love is your love. The songs you come across and play on repeat for days, weeks, or months, are yours. The books you discover hidden behind the rest on the shelves are yours to keep. Those worlds are yours. You can be selfish with all of it because it is yours. Fall in love with these things and do it all without remorse, for you are falling in love with yourself and that, my sweet, is the best gem you'll ever stumble upon.

Wendy's Woods

There is a forest in my chest. It sways when I am happy, when I am calm, and when I am in an absolutely careless and euphoric state. These are the feelings that often complete me. There is a match and suddenly my forest is ablaze. The fire spreads when I am stressed or tense or having a mental breakdown. But when I breath so deeply that I can feel it reach the roots of these trees, I am slowly intoxicating myself and putting the fire out. When I slow myself and the world around me with someone's melodic voice echoing in my ears, the fire fades.

Dear You (Someday)

Dear Future Husband,

I hope you are doing okay. I hope you are living. I hope you are learning. I hope you are loving and caring and being as good a human being as any. As you can see, I have a lot of hopes for you. But most of all, I hope you know that I am waiting for you. And waiting does not mean putting the rest of my life on pause. Waiting means living and learning and loving and caring and feeling emotions and doing all of those things so that I may have experiences. I am living with the expectation of meeting you someday, wherever and whoever you may be. I'm living so that when "someday" arrives, I'll have stories to tell you. I hope you're doing the same. I hope you'll share it all with me when "someday" comes.

Love, Future Wife .xx

Dear You (Someday) Cont'd.

Sidebar:

I can't wait to tell you about all the times I thought of you. I knew you, I fell in love with you and with our future without even knowing who you were or what your name was. Yet, you were always in the back of my mind and on nights like this you were the only one I thought about. It is December 29, 2017 at 12:47 a.m. and I know that I love you. I don't even need to be near you to love you. I am probably the farthest from your thoughts at this moment in time and that is perfectly okay because one day you'll love me as much as I do you, and by then we'll know each other so well that no cold winds could blow out our burning flames.

- *Our love is one that does not flicker, my dear.*

Third Times A Charm

You with your melodies that sent me right into a peaceful bliss, even over FaceTime, even when the connection cut out.

You were the first boy who ever stayed on video chat with me and watched me fall asleep, and was still there when I woke up.

You gave me a set of standards, you were the basis for the rest that would follow.

Give Give Give. Eventually you will be given. This is what you deserve, but just keep on giving for their regular amount of nothing in return.

~~You~~ taught me to give more of myself than he did, to share more of myself than you or any boy every would share in return with me.

Maybe if I shared enough, if I gave enough, I would finally have something concrete.

~~You~~ taught me that there are no promises in kisses, actions don't always speak louder than words because if they did, you and I would have been <u>something</u> by now.

~~You~~ said you wanted nothing and yet you held me in your arms like I was something. was something.

Your actions said more about your character

than my naiveness.

All I did was *give give give* to the three of you.
The three that I will always dismiss as two,
because I don't want to believe that I truly gave
so much of myself.
You were the three that taught me that
people *take take take* without end, without
remorse.
When will the silly little girl learn to stop
giving?
To stop saying "it's okay" when she knows
it's not?

Magnetic Poetry

So spring
From this
Moon
And
Glow
My Love

An ache
Of void
Must do
More than
Scream to
Heal Me

I Broke My Own Heart

I am addicted to the sadness. I can delve into my past and pick it apart piece by piece, minute by minute. I am addicted to my self-deprecating tendencies. I can revisit every hurtful word I spoke to or about myself and feel the pain all over again with an odd sense of pleasure; perhaps pleasure that others will be happy to view my suffering. I am addicted to the four walls I build around myself. Each brick is laid by my conflicting thoughts, the screams of anger and self-loathing in my head, and the damage others have done to me that will never equal the amount I do to myself.

- *I built a fortress with a broken heart*

Eros & Agape

I have come to know Eros love and Agape has yet to find me. I find Eros in his slender fingers gliding along my cheek. I find Eros in the pull of his lips, the grasp of his hands in my hair. Eros makes herself known in the way he cannot promise to love me, but the way he kisses me like he wants to. Eros is in the way he calls me "friend", in the way he signs his letters "love, your friend". Eros sits him on a high throne of lost lovers and bows down at his feet. Eros is fast, impulsive, and temporary. Agape may be waltzing down a lonesome avenue, forming pairs as she goes. Agape is in the slow, relaxed press of lips, laughs of happy souls at midnight dancing in refrigerator lights. Agape hides herself in the way he writes her notes everyday professing his never-ending love, the simple tone of understanding as he listens to her vent about her hardships. Agape needs no throne, no pedestal, no worship; She seeks only unconditional commitment when there is nothing to give and nothing to take. Agape places them miles apart in an orchard of tall apple trees with wolves and peril weather in between. Agape is slow, calm, and permanent, and I, in my restless patience, am waiting for her to get to me while Eros has her way.

Words are better than any boy will ever be,
but I didn't account for what happened with the
words you said to me.

Feening

Month 1: You dismissed it as nothing, a
simple crush without promise of more.
Month 2: It became something, and the
weight grew in your heart as you stood and
listened to the waves crash against the shore.
Month 3: The effort began; You begged,
pleaded, and acted on pure desire.
Month 4: You were granted your wish, and in
your heart the heavy weight was followed by an
intense fire.
Month 5: God forbid you call it love, for it
was not that at all, but the way lips contacted
lips, hands ran through hair, you found it hard
not to fall.
Month 6: You stressed, cried, and vented to
your friends who could not bear to see you
chase
Month 7: Ditch the extra heartache,
Are you forgetting who you are,
Doll Face?

I always have such lovely evenings, but still
wind up with heartbroken feelings.

- *It takes more than lovers to break my heart*

Is It Enough?

If I say it late at night
when you're half asleep and dreaming,
Will you know how much I care,
how much I am utterly feening?
If I say it in a hurry
with one foot out the door,
Will you be satisfied
Or will you ask for more?
If I say it in the good mornings, good nights,
And all the get home safes,
Will you return the decency
or let me alone crave?
Because I need you to know the way I want you
And the way I need you,
I need you to know the words I am scared to say
For fear of losing you once I do.

- ~~*I love you*~~ 3/29/18 1:25 AM

When we were younger and the grown-ups
told us we could become whatever we wanted to
be, I don't think they ever anticipated the
practicality of things or our broken economy.

Who am I to pretend I was innocent? We were both partially darkened souls and we saw in each other the parts of ourselves we didn't like, so we reflected our sadness and anger and shifted the blame. And then, my dear, we both played the victim. So who was really wrong and who was really right?

- *Trick Question*

My French Boy

The boy in the back of my mind. He's the one I go to after I've had my heart broken or when I am lonely, but still happy, and yet sad all at once. The life that I live with him is something far away.

In this imaginary life we live in his apartment in Brooklyn. He's one for the arts; He plays guitar and paints and loves photography and videography.

We are in a kind of love that is so easy, yet deep and somehow just from this fantasy I can tell that it is unconditional, that he is my one and only, my forever and always. I wear his button down shirt that is oversized on me, and in the mornings when he makes the pancakes and I make the coffee we dance so carelessly. He twirls me, and even then, when we are acting so child-like, I know he loves me.

He constantly takes pictures of me because I am something he doesn't want to forget, that he wants to capture forever in these irrevocable moments in time. He takes pictures of me simply living: when I read in the park leaning against a tree, when I brush my teeth, when I am doing my makeup, when I am singing unconsciously.

I know the songs that we dance to, or rather live to, it is like a montage or a music video in my head.

I believe this boy is a combination of all the random strangers I have come across and found attractive in one way or another.

He is the French boy at the dentist's office, he is the boy who was staring at me in the Union Square shop that my sister noticed and I didn't, he is the boy in the magazine isle at Barnes and Noble, he is the one behind me in the Starbucks line, he is the one studying and secretly listening to my conversation with my friends outside of a coffee shop in June.

The best of this is that he loves me the way I love him or maybe even more so.

I Care Too Much

It's funny that the things that once meant nothing to me now hold so much meaning because I've met you. It's hard to forget someone when you see them all around you.

It Hit Me

When I first met you we had little to nothing in common. I suppose someone had hurt you before and you decided to close off your heart. Maybe meeting you happened too soon. You probably saw something in me that had been completely unaffected by the same pain that you had felt. You thought you could fix or change me, that you were helping me grow. You projected the part of yourself that was in pain onto me. By the end of it, we finally had something in common.

- *We're not so different anymore* 1/12/18

Sometimes I am blind. I am blind to love or I
am blind to hate. I am so lost that it takes me a
while before I can find my way back to
normalcy, if there even is such a thing.

Irony

I was sitting on the floor of my bedroom having an emotional breakdown about my weight and appearance for about twenty minutes, just crying my soul out. When I was nearly done I stood up and looked in the mirror, my face wet with tears, hair flat and oily, and thought that this was the most raw and beautiful I have ever seen myself.

Show Me

I feel like an accident of nature
Is this really who I am meant to be?
Show me your plan, where have you written it?
I need to know that I am not an experiment gone wrong
How insignificant will I be?
In 50 years from now? In 20 or 100 years after I die?
You show me these people whose talents have been harvested from youth, but where are mine?
Am I even capable of creating something as beautiful and wondrous as they have?
Will I be remembered for something like they will?
I ask again, what is your plan for me?

I would like to say that I am happy with the person I am, the person I am becoming. But on nights like this when the sadness sits on my chest so heavy and draining with almost parasitic behavior, I cannot find the happiness or hope within me.

- *And here I thought I was Gatsby*

Forgiveness is in my bones.
Love runs through my veins.
I was born into a world of hate and
Whether they knew it or not,
I eventually became aware.
The atoms I am made up of are armed.
I am not as holy as a temple,
However I am as strong as a fortress.
So I warn you not to mistake my kindness
for weakness.
I will give you a second chance, a third, a
fourth, a fifth,
Until you have bled me dry.
The fact still remains that every time you
betray my trust, I am gutted.

If your love was like credit but you said you had no money left in the bank, did you think I was stupid? I know how credit works, dearest. You had love to give, you just weren't willing.

- *How dare you take me for a fool.*

I hate the ache that ensues when I feel like crying but no tears will fall. It's as if they are afraid to touch my cheeks, as if they know they will be dried faster than they fell. Because I am stronger now than I ever was before.

Little girls are supposed to learn how a man
should act and treat them from their fathers.
I guess that means that a man should lie,
scream, bicker, make false promises, steal, give
half-assed apologies, and have no moral
compass. Maybe that's why I'm so attracted to
the boys who treat me like I have no worth.

- *Who needs a therapist when I can psychoanalyze myself?*

4/16/18

Maybe if I had someone to do the loving for me I wouldn't feel so empty most of the time.

4/9/18 12:23 AM

That aching, heavy weight in your chest, the one that strikes out of nowhere and drawls on for what feels like an eternity. That's the feeling you get when reality comes knocking at your door. When you feel like you have your life in order, everything nice and neat and scheduled, you'll have a new house guest that will clumsily break all of your shelves and you're back to the mess you started with. It came for me one night when I thought I was safe, when I was happy, and it hurt me in a way that every teenager must be hurt when they understand that they have a dream they cannot reach for any longer. I am sixteen and this is a heartbreak I know all too well.

4/9/18 8:59 PM

I can do whatever I damn well please. All it took was someone telling me to choose the more stable and comfortable lifestyle over the way I really want to live, with risks, to awaken my incentive. They didn't have to say the words "you can't do it", it was in the way they chose stability over my wildest dreams. But I'm coming for them anyway.

4/18/18 11:49 PM

I went to an Ed Sheeran concert when I was thirteen and it was one of the best experiences of my life. It's often the soundtrack of my life. I can still feel the beat in my chest, it is the beat that made me feel alive, the beat that I will forever feel in my heart.

4/25/18 9:41 PM

I tried to keep a bullet journal where I tracked my emotions for this whole year and so far I already notice more gray days than yellow ones. By the end of my time on this earth I can only hope and pray I conclude with more happy days than sad.

Consistencies

Baby blue, faded, criss-crossed blankie that I
seek comfort in, no matter how old I get.
Grandma-gifted Guyana gold bent bangle on
my brown wrist that knocks against the surface
when I write, that I instinctively wave my hand
around to slide back up my arm even if it's not
on, that I will rarely ever take off.
Piled up comforters over my stomach to hide
my insecurities, no matter how hot the weather
might be.
Fairy lights on as I sleep, rosary above my
bed, Hawaii on my right that used to transport
me to a life different than my own.
Evan, just Evan. What is life without him?
Gramma and Grampa, their ever-loving,
ever-giving, ever-comforting presence.
Mommy working, Daddy driving, Kimmy
studying.
Endless family celebrations with the Aunties
and Uncles and Cousins.
God instilled for longer than I can
remember, I don't even recall when I knew who
He was or what He meant to me.

I'll Know

The day that I ask myself "If he were to show up right now and ask me to be his, would I say yes?" and the answer is finally no, that's how I'll know that I'm over you.

Lately I've been having a hard time feeling good enough. I cannot seem to find my worth. I look for it in my SAT scores, my grades, my weight, my wealth status. All of these are things that people my age in this time period should know don't define your worth or value, and when I'm thinking clearly I do know this. So how come when I'm thinking to myself, these are the thoughts that arise, the ones that have been ingrained into my mind?

Le Marais

The sound of a piano is like a breath of fresh air to me. It is the sound of coming home and the sound of the life I could have lived (once upon a time ago…)

My heart will always swoon for it and for anyone who plays it for me. This sound will send me back: six years old holding my mother's hand and walking into the room of pianos lined up in rows, a personal heaven for each child that played, and feeling like this was the place I was meant to be. Yes, the sound that was instilled in me, I will always remember the positioning of my hands on the keys without quite remembering who it was that taught it to me in the first place, but I will know for certain that it is home. My piano, you are the one I will always come back to, no matter how many years may pass, I escape in you.

I'll swear that I don't care about you or that you don't mean anything to me. But no one loses sleep over things they don't care about. In the morning my tiredness will be a reminder of you.

If you ever lose me, you can come find me in
these poems.

Living feels like a chore.
- 5/27/18 1:19 PM

Moment of Weakness

I just want to be beautiful. I want to have fit arms and legs that are clear and smooth and a flat stomach and a smaller face and no cellulite and no dark knees or underarms. I want to have money so I can buy a new house and clothes for my beautiful dream body and a car and pay for school and pursue my dreams and travel and just *live*, God I just want to ***live***.

When I say "I love you" I am going off of the presumption that I know what love is. When I say "I want to die" I am going off of the presumption that death is better than my current situation.

Golden Tears

I feel so far away, so dissociated from my friends, from love, and from trust. I feel close to sadness, anxiety, anger, pain. Yet, wasn't I just with three of my friends no less than two hours ago? They are there when life is easy, but I cannot run to them when I need to cry on one of their shoulders, to no fault of their own. It is me, it is the sadness and anxiety and anger and pain in my head, and I am sorry that I must be coming off as distant to them. But I miss them, and I miss myself, however I know this is just me growing. I first must cry into my own being before I lean on another.

- 6/3/18 DUMBO

My dad always said "See you later" whenever I said "Bye", whether it be when he dropped me off at school, home, or a sleepover. He was the only person who refused to say any form of "Goodbye" that wasn't his "See you later", because he knew it was never really goodbye. The first time I was with you and I had to leave I said "Bye" and you said "See you later", and it felt so strange to hear it from someone who wasn't him. You both were so similar, you always knew it wasn't goodbye, you were fighters, and that wasn't always a bad thing. But you both broke pieces of my heart in one way or another and that is what I will remember the most.

Old Habits Die Hard

Does it ever occur to you that no one knows the last time will be the last time? Or maybe they have an idea, but they are proven wrong. The last time I drank a Gatorade, the last time I played Freeze Tag, the last time I saw one of my elementary school teachers, the last time I saw you. I thought it was in my control. I wanted to seal the thought of you and everything that happened with you in a crimson colored envelope, carefully place it in a hat box, and bury it under the billions of grains of sand under the Mariana Trench. But it wasn't over then and it isn't over now, no matter how much I'd like to deny it. You're the bad habit I cannot seem to kick.

Money is Everything

"It's nice to have money"
"Wow how come people have money like that?"
"Why can't we make money?"
"When you don't have money in life it's such an unsaid crime."

Carnivore

More is what you wanted them to want from you. You wanted them to ask for the same "more" that you weren't able to. It was always on the tip of your tongue but you never let it slip, as if it were cotton candy you were trying to save from disintegrating, because once it left your mouth it would be irretrievable.
I want more – in the form of kisses, cuddles, and "I love you"s
I want more – when you reply with emojis or give me one word answers
I want more – when you're standing right beside me but you feel so far away
They wanted more, but not in the way you wanted at all. They wanted more of what you thought would please them, satisfy them, and forever give you their attention. They wanted more of what you set out on platters for them to eat, so how could you be mad when they asked for seconds?
I want more – in the form of riskier details in our messages
I want more – when it is late at night and I know you are up and will come running at my beck and call
Silly girl, when will you learn – you placed fresh, beautiful foliage and raw, bloody meat in front of the wolves and were surprised when they ravaged through the choice that was less appeasing to you, but undeniably satisfying to them.

Mr. Moon

At night when I stand by the window the world
looks as if it has paused. The moon is full and
pale, shadowed by the trees. I remember when I
was younger and it was the same moon I stared
at while in the car driving someplace. It
followed me then and it follows me now.
Dear moon, you must remember me, don't you?
You know me because I know you. All those
years ago I wanted to travel to you, feel your
surface, and become your friend for eternity.
Some of my love is lost now, my innocence and
hope, and you must know this to be true
because the trees will whisper my name filled
with sorrow loud enough for even you to hear.

"So Sit Here and Try To Remember It"

The harrowing truth is that this will pass and you will never be able to live it over again. No matter if the situation is extremely good or terribly bad, it will pass and nothing will ever be the same as it was in that moment. I can feel it slipping from me now, I can feel myself in twenty years or so thinking back on this time of my life and wondering how I let it leave me so quickly. I know there is no use crying about it now and the only thing left to do is enjoy it in the moment as it is, but oh, how I wish to just freeze time and remember it exactly like *this*, forever, without end. This is the way I live and love and cry and anger and laugh.

Haiku for Mum

I love my mommy
I owe her the world and more
How much can I give?

Lucky

How lucky am I! I have never known what it is like to grieve/mourn or deal with death, and if I have it was very briefly with relatives I hardly remember and thus I was barely affected by. I wish it would stay that way, but I know as time goes on death and grief grow closer on their search to entrap me and on this night, I am utterly afraid. I would willingly die before any one of my family members, which speaks volumes on exactly how selfish I am; that I would die before I would experience the pain or grief because I know, *I know*, it would break me more than anything else ever could.

When I was a kid I didn't understand how people got married, I wanted to cry at the thought of even moving in with a stranger and leaving my parents forever. But what 8-year-old me didn't understand was that I wouldn't be moving in with a stranger, I would be moving in with the man I loved which automatically made him family. I would never have to leave my parents either, the distance I go from them is entirely up to me and my future husband. As my future becomes more and more uncertain with each passing day, the thought of the man who will someday become part of my family is something I grow certain in with time.

You're too scared to take a risk on yourself and
on your dream. Do you know how ridiculous
that sounds given you are the adventurer of
your group? The one who never hesitates to
venture into the unknown.

You and I are hardly two ships passing in the night, rather you are the ship on its steady course in the ocean and I am the plane far above you watching, waiting, knowing we shall never meet, lest I crash and call upon you to rescue me.

- *Destruction is our only connection*

I like the sound of the rain. I like the smell it forms when it comes in contact with grass: Petrichor. The soft *tip-tap* it makes against the window at night is like the call of an eager old friend who wants to know how I've been. The rain misses me and I miss it as well. It is no longer sad the way it was in the winter, the way it poured fiercely and angrily. It is sweet, gentle summer rain and it is the best kind of all.

- 7/22/18 12:01 AM

Two Weeks Is Long Enough

New York! I'm home! My heart leaps in excitement in my chest, I immediately let out a deep sigh of relief. I see the first signs of my city below me and the simple sight is so comforting. No longer am I suspended between real, hustling life and unsure, too-calm vacation schedule. I am home at last, it has been far too long. I am back where the buildings stand tall and surround the highways jammed with traffic, where the city hums a tune of fast-paced life and exudes the harmonizing dynamics of a busy population. I cannot stop smiling, my heart cannot stop leaping, and all I can think is *I'm home!*

Every night I talk to God
And it feels the same
He must already know what I'm going to say
I bet he knows how I've been wasting my days.

I've come to realize that I want things in a
manner that I hold sand in the palm of my hand
– I desire these things so much and am so
scared of losing them that when the wind blows,
I squeeze until I open my hand to see it was my
own doing that made it leave.

I'm scared to fall asleep, to shut my eyes and
miss the many happenings of the world. While I
go silent and my body lies still, I am unaware of
the events around me: a baby might be nuzzling
against her mother looking for a place to rest
her head, a party might be getting louder down
the street, lovers may be reconciling over a fight
that requires damage control. All this and so
much more, but if I let my eyes fall how will I
ever know any of it?

- *I'm only human*

There's a house in New York,
And inside there's a girl.
She sits inside reading
And waiting for the world to fall at her feet.
But one day she's tired of waiting and decides to leave her house.
She travels to the city trying to seek out something with meaning, something with purpose, something worth feeling.
On the first day she goes to the city it doesn't come,
"Well of course it wouldn't", she thinks,
"It's only day one."
So she travels again on odd days with her friends and they're all in search of fun, but never in the exact way she is, never in the hunt for magic that she is.
After a while she wonders if maybe waiting would've been a better choice, to let the universe decide when it was ready for her.
"But no", she thinks, "this is my life and I have the right to take control of it."
So it is a constant dance between her and Fate and Searching, with the world hanging in the balance.
Sometimes the dance becomes vicious, and Searching grabs the girl to run after Fate, but Fate is much too clever and always outsmarts them.
There's a house in New York,
And inside there's a girl – sometimes she's reading, sometimes she's waiting, sometimes she's out searching
For all the magic of the world.

Ghosted

You were in my mind last night. I saw you before I fell asleep. So how is it that I wake up and you are nowhere to be found, have you so easily forgotten me?

Body

Shower her with love.
Treat her with respect.
Show her off, show some skin, and ignore when they tell you to cover up.
Because she is yours and she deserves to be paraded around.
Strut in her with your head held high and let your confidence soar.
Let her know that you appreciate her,
That you are proud of her and wouldn't dare
Hide her from the world.
She does so much for you,
So much to keep you alive,
So make sure you do all this to honor her
And return the favor.

- *I love you, scars and all*

Sadist

Look at me and see placid
Look at me and see oblivious
Look at me and see ignorant
Know that I feel psychotic
Know that on the inside I am ripping myself apart
With my bare teeth
My hands quiver not even in the slightest
But on the inside the wolves have come
Tearing, shredding, grabbing, biting
But we know the wolves are me and I am them
Eyes glistening at the sight of damage
And blood because
Inside me this is real
What I feel and will not show
But you must know
Know it when you look at me
See vacant, but know I am leaping with pain
Unafraid to destroy myself
From the inside alone.

Eyes glossed over
Wet pages
Heart torn
Blasting ear drums
The knife is already in,
Won't you be a dear and twist it deeper?

My body aches and screams out to me
Because of the way I lay.
My side contracts and churns in rebellion
Because it refuses to be stretched out in this way.
My legs and stomach and arms throb and
I know by the way I can see the movement
Even from underneath my skin
That they are revolting against me.
But I do not listen and instead I press
Harder into my sides with the blanket that I lay on.
My body screams louder now,
But I do not listen.
Because for now this is my reason to cry
My reason to feel
My reason to be anything but numb.

Why do my days slip past me? Why do they rush by? Are they aware of something better to come, something that I must hurry to see? Why must I fight them to savor and revel in these small moments? It feels like a repeatedly infinitesimal early death every time.

I mixed myself a cup of lemon and honey
Because I thought it would take away the pain
Of screaming for your attention.

When we were in elementary school and they taught us about God, they would tell us that even though we can't see him he's always there. The same can be said about my love for you: even when I think it has left me, even when I can't see it or there is no proof of it, it is always there in one form or another.

In the morning dew I can remember you
Reassuring me,
"We'll still talk, I'm certain."
In the afternoon heat I listen to your pretty lies,
Because I'd rather have falsities
Than none of you at all.
In the desperate night we whisper slow
goodbyes,
Knowing that what we had is no more.
But the wind sings a different song,
And although this has all gone wrong
I wouldn't trade any of it for the world.

I'm tired
Of the crescents in my palms & thighs
Of the faded cat scratches on my left forearm
Of the *I can't I can't I can't* echoing in my head
Of the scream I can feel but will not reign out
Of the saltwater I can taste on my tongue
Of my heart beating faster than I care to count
Of the pounding in my head
Of the recurring of it all
And one day I hope it
Just
Stops

If you had all the world right on your fingertips,
right in front of your eyes, there is no mistaking
it. It'll come to life before you and all that
history has made of it will now become part of
your memories forever. Let it bloom and let
yourself fly free with it.

There are so many questions I want to ask you.
If you were an animal, which one would you be?
If you were a color, which one would you be?
Do you believe in the theories I believe in? Let's discuss.
I want my mind to spin and dance, rise and fall,
with the idea of you cascading around me.
Let's talk about music and art, tell me what your
life has been like before me, I want to know all
of you because I want you to know all of me…

My worst fear is falling into a relationship like
theirs,
Becoming him.

Chandany

I grew up with the moon
God only knows how fast my moods change
I've always felt its phantom touch within me
I am the loneliest of wolves
Howling out for my greatest connection
Knowing I can never reach it.

You grew up with the moon & now you're such a wolf, howling out for it. It's why you're Chandany.

When I find myself, there will be no looking back. We will run away together, as we deserve to, because we have taken far too long to cross each other's paths. I am a husk and pieces of my soul are wandering lost, wild, and free looking for me.

I am here! Just a little longer!

I cannot wait to feel whole at last.

- 9/12/18 11:30 PM

I can feel my sobs stuck in my throat. The painful way I choke on them. A scream dissipating between my teeth and tongue. I can't even comprehend anything other than this moment. There is no future. "There is a God" Where is your God now? I feel myself about to pull the trigger on my words. But I have to remember that my tongue is glass and if these words slip, there's nothing left for me to do but shatter. This music is loud, and I'll probably pay for it in the future, but it's still not loud enough to drown out everything else. No one is here to fix me or superglue me back together, nonetheless I feel myself cracking. No one is here, no one was here before, and no one will ever be here to pick up the pieces; No one except for me. Lord help me, I can feel my humanity teetering over the abyss.

- 9/14/18 10:28 PM

"She's Traveling Now"

Place the lime & lemon underneath your pillow,
Buy your quicksilver soon.
Ask for forgiveness and reflect on what was,
because it is now no longer.
I will watch for you in a shadow passing across
the next full moon,
I will listen for you in the whistling of the wind
through the crack of my window.
If I had known I would not see you in this
lifetime again I would've found my way back to
you sooner.
Rest Easy & Know You Were Loved

I want you to stay
But it feels like you'll leave
And I can't afford any more tainted memories.

Happy Seventeen

I don't mind the wrinkles when I remember all
the smiles and laughter that came with them
Just as I don't mind the cuts on the back of my
ankles when I remember the lot of us bolting up
train station stairs with crouched knees in heels.

At first I wanted to, I really did.
It was impulsive & I should've listened to my

voice of reason.
But I didn't expect it to go as bad as it did.
Why were you so insistent?
Come back. It'll be worth your while :)
It was like everything I'd learned from the stories of others vanished from my mind.
Okay.
Why did I say that? I was anything but that.
Maybe I thought it could get better, that you'd be sweeter, like the version I'd daydreamed of for so long.
It didn't.
I forgot how to say *no*
Where was my stubbornness when I needed it most?
And then I was scared,
Scared to upset you. To make you sad or angry.
Scared of what you would do to me.
But there was no use in being scared,
Because you'd already corrupted the part of me I didn't want you to touch.
It's turned black now, it's started to rot.
The part of me I started to love? You pushed her out.
She must feel betrayed.
I'm waiting for her to come back and touch the rotten black, waiting for her to make it gold and vibrant again.
I need her.
I've never needed you.

When you hear these words I hope you think of me.
Dream of me and of how I was before I left you
Before I stole your soul
Before I stole your hope
Before I drained you
I hope you think of me and of how I took everything from you
I hope you feel it all over again
I hope you feel my hands playing around in your brain
And my smile, the smile that did it
I hope you feel the excruciating cold air blowing through the windows,
The kind that only comes from the icy depths of hell,
Because when that place freezes over
You'll know that it was me that did it.

- *I am your cold day in hell*

You think that it's love when you wake up at 3 a.m. to screaming back and forth.
You think that it's love – those plastered up holes in the wall caused by either a shoe or a fist (you're not really certain).
You think that it's love when "I'm calling the cops" is a phrase heard much too often.
You think that it's love when they're calling out for you through sobs to do something.
You think that it's love – that splintered door frame, broken as a force into an equally broken home.
You think that it's love when you hear the loud footsteps paired with loud voices, the crashing of objects in their path.
You think that it's love when you wake up to screaming at 6 a.m. on a Tuesday right before school, or at 8 a.m. on a Sunday when all you want is to sleep in.
You think that it's love until you realize it can't be – love cannot present itself in the sound of your music getting louder in your ears to mask the screams, in your heart racing with anxiety, in the impulsive thoughts racing through your mind trying to find a quick escape, in the betrayal, in the lies, in the forced happiness.
I hope you learn that love is not the bringer of pain,
I hope you hold onto that hope.

- 12/9/18 11:50 PM

Bourbon and Grapes

What more can I say?
I wonder if it was a promise as empty as you made me feel
When you left and promised we'd still be friends.
When you returned, my heart felt heavy,
Not with love but with anxiety
"Bourbon and grapes?"
I say as I am still hurting
As if I am reaching out to feel what once was
But I was right
And it was empty
And so am I

- 12/18/18 12:03 AM

Sometimes I forget that people are a blessing
They can be the sanity you need
When all you feel is absolutely drained
You can channel happiness from them
Use them for support
And they might not even know it,
But they're tethering you to this world.

- *I need you more than you need me, Merry Christmas Class of 2019*

When I think about the words and thoughts I
want to voice out loud
I think of the inside of my mind.
There's a little me running around in the
darkness,
Searching through the hollow walls
But once you get lost on one end,
You don't find your way back to the start.
- 12/21/18 4:43 PM

Cont'd

The words, my thoughts, trailing along the walls
My hand pressed against it, trying to rip it from the surface
Eyes straining in the darkness to see more than a few words.
And so I let my hand drag on across the never ending walls,
Grabbing and digging until the paint is peeling
And sheet rock dust is stuck underneath my nail beds.

Long Way From Home

You didn't drift this time
You ran and hid
From me.
I think at first you were scared
But now it's just a Game
And sometimes I can hear you giggling
In excitement
Because you're ready for me to find you
Again.
This time is different
You're a long way from home, honey
And although this is childish
When I find you, we'll be better for it.
- 1/2/19 2:40 PM

1:49 AM

I can't fall asleep
When I know she's out.
How would I live
Knowing the last thing she said was
"I'll be home at 1"
Knowing the last thing I said was
"Okay"
Where that one word holds the silent promise
That I will wait up for the sound of her keys
jangling in the hallway
Of her fiddling with the small black padlock on
her door.
I can't even bring myself to try to sleep,
My mind will jolt me awake.
Because I am my sister's keeper
And I will be until the end of my days.

I thought about texting you one night
Late
And telling you that I missed you.
But I didn't want you to think that I only miss you
When nothing else is plaguing my mind.
Because the truth is that you're always in my thoughts
Even in the busiest moment of my day.
I never stop thinking about you
And, God, how I wish I would.
I don't miss you only at night
I don't miss you only when I'm lonely
I would love to play it off as that
Because that would be so much easier.
But I miss you
When I'm drinking coffee and the sugar isn't as sweet as you
When I'm skating and every boy in hockey skates reminds me of you
When I'm walking in the city and every Rangers jersey makes me want to talk to you
When I'm daydreaming of a different life and the face of the boy is yours.
I miss you and I hate that I miss you and I wish I would learn to
Just
Stop
Missing
You.

New York Minute

Why are you always running off somewhere?
You're always pacing
You can never sit still
Your knees are always shaking
(Even without the caffeine)
Your mind is always screaming
And you can feel it even when you're sleeping.
I guess that's what happens
When you grow up
In a city
Where no one ever stops moving.

"I am going to stay up all night to do this and then pump my body full of caffeine in the morning and hope for the best."

- *Result of Procrastination*

Teenager

I'm scared
I'm angry
I'm sad
I'm anxious
I'm in love
I'm happy
I'm excited
I am a whirlwind of emotions
And I am loving every second of it.
- *Block 6* 10:58 AM

When I was little I used to think that every bad thing that happened to me or the people around me was my fault. Because right before it happened, I usually had done something for myself or acted selfish. But I was about eight, so what the hell did I know about being selfish?

It took me a while to learn that bad things just happen and most of the time they are out of my control. It isn't my fault.
In turn, it took me a while to stop feeling guilty. But it comes back every now and then, the guilt. And it's like teaching myself over again that it isn't my fault and that bad things happen all the time.

- 1/19/19 1:00 AM

If you are in pain, you must have loved.
You must have been loved.
- 1/31/19 5:43 PM

I must not be the only one when I say that
September feels like a million light years away.
- 1/31/19 9:37 PM

I've always wanted to "vlog" my life so that
when I got older I could look back on all the
lessons I've learned and experiences I've had. I
guess I've somewhat done that through my
writing, and realizing that is one of the best
feelings I've felt in a long time.

I write for the kids in the backseat
Because I am a kid in the backseat
Caught in the daydreams
Lost in thought
Eyes roaming the mountains and leafless trees
Up to the faint drifting clouds and airplane streaks in the sky
Until I catch the same wandering eyes
Of a kid in the backseat
Just like me
I write to tell that kid that I see them
And hear them
And I know they exist
That their daydreams are not pointless
That they mean something.

- 2/2/19 2:26 PM

I like the way he calls me “nana”
Because he’s the only one that says it
And it’s just for him
I like the way he hears my real name
And laughs
Like I’m just joking with him
Laughs in that little kid laugh that makes everything else seem ridiculous
Because he’s certain that I’m just “nana”
I hope he never stops calling me that
I hope he never forgets it

Heartbeat

The sound you hear rushing through your ears
when you're in fight or flight mode.
It's a constant in a world of chaos.
If you close your eyes and leave your hand on
your chest,
Or two fingers on your wrist right under your
thumb,
it does wonders in reassuring you
That you are alive
And that thought alone can bring me back
Keep me centered
When all else fails.

Radius & Ulna

These days it seems as though you and I are like
the radius and the ulna, twisting around each
other so harmoniously, running on parallel fates,
and yet always separated in the ways that matter
the most.

Neverland

I awoke with a start from a slumber I thought would never end
Half past noon as I groggily made my way out of bed
And through a tunnel I encountered a town of unknown
Where the world looked different
Like a fairytale from a storybook come to life
Blue skies stretched out for miles, clocktower in the center of town, groups of unaccompanied children running about, smiles all around
And as I walk through so in awe
A part of me hopes that I run into Peter Pan
That he invites me to stay forever
And tells me it's where I was meant to be
All along

Ready

I can see my future
It's that zig-zagging path
That's sometimes foggy and has too many road signs to follow
I can hear the music and the laughter
The cries and screams of desperation and sorrow
And all the uncertainty that lies in between
But right now
I feel the anxiety coiled with excitement bubbling within me
And it lets me know
I am ready

The fact is that my brain is absolutely flooded
With thoughts I cannot find words for
But so desperately want to say
So instead I will wait for the day
The doubt flees from my mind
And all that is left is pure conviction
Because then
Then
My words will not escape me

Midnight

In the hours after Midnight
I become inspired
Because when everyone and everything is silent
There is nothing stopping the world
From singing life into my ears
In a way it was not able to
In broad daylight.

New Moon

"Today was weird for me, was today weird for you?"
Today everything felt different and I didn't know why.
Today everything felt heightened,
Like life was running at me with full force,
Like everything wanted to be seen and heard.
It felt like the world was slowing down
And allowing me to take in every feeling that needed to be felt and every sight that needed to be seen.
As if I was doing a lifetime of living in a simple day,
The universe called out to me.
By the time I saw the purple sky begin to set, by the time I questioned the light scattering, I realized something had happened today.
And now I know,
With the waning crescent of the moon here to assure me,
That this is where I end before I start anew.
This is where the rest of the living begins.

Acknowledgements

Thank you to my parents, Indy and Neal, for letting me wander the world and learn life lessons from the moment I could walk. You've gifted me with experience.

To my sister, Kimberly. Because of you I will always have someone to come home to, to look out for, to jam in the car with, and tell my stories to, no matter how late at night it is.

To Evan – my favorite boy in the entire universe. You gifted me with responsibility. I love you "a million much" too.

To Trisha. You are the Sun to my Moon & my role model. My trust in you is infinite. How lucky am I to have found a best friend in my own family? Fate really knew what she was doing with us.

To Karina. I will never be alone in this world because I have you. We are bonded by more than friendship, there is no word for us. We grow together, learn together, and always make it right back to each other. We are the destined stars.

To my friends – Daphne, Victoria, Maria, Alisha, Laura, Ashley W., Ashley D., - and many more I have not the space to name (it would surely take up a page). Through late night video chats, texts, and loud conversations in class or

the halls, you never fail to support and love me.
You mean the world to me.

To Madison – for being a brilliant friend and for designing the cover.

To Ms. Shannon – my favorite English teacher and the first to believe in my writing.

To Ms. Forlini for taking me on as a mentee and believing in this project.

To Gingerbread Boy and Bourbon & Grapes– I would not be writing this without the experiences I had with you. Consider us even.

ABOUT THE AUTHOR

Breanna Chandany Shievdayal is a seventeen year old writer born and raised in Bronx, New York. While attending college next fall as a nursing major, she hopes to pursue her writing and follow wherever it may lead.

Social Media:

Instagram: @b.c.shiev

Twitter: @BCShiev

Made in the USA
Middletown, DE
21 May 2019